CANINE CAREERS
Dogs at Work

BOOKS BY JUDITH SCHODER

Brotherhood of Pirates

Canine Careers
  Dogs at Work

CANINE CAREERS
Dogs at Work

by JUDITH SCHODER

Illustrated with photographs

JULIAN MESSNER New York

Copyright © 1981 by Judith Schoder

All rights reserved including the right of reproduction in whole or in part in any form. Published by Julian Messner, a Simon & Schuster Division of Gulf & Western Corporation, Simon & Schuster Building, 1230 Avenue of the Americas, New York, New York 10020. JULIAN MESSNER and colophon are trademarks of Simon & Schuster, registered in the U.S. Patent and Trademark Office.

Manufactured in the United States of America.

Design by Stanley S. Drate

Library of Congress Cataloging in Publication Data

Schoder, Judith.
   Canine careers.

   Includes index.
   Summary: Discusses the careers for which dogs have been trained and their work as hunters, shepherds, guides for the handicapped, lifeguards, detectives, friends and companions, etc.
   1. Working dogs—Juvenile literature. [1. Working dogs. 2. Dogs] I. Title.
SF428.2.S36   636.7'3   81-11029
ISBN 0-671-41907-2   AACR2

Dedication

To my best four-footed friends—
past, present, and future.

CONTENTS

1	In The Beginning	*11*
2	Hunting Dogs	*18*
3	Sled Dogs	*27*
4	Seeing-Eye and Hearing-Ear Dogs	*35*
5	Search and Rescue Dogs	*45*
6	Lifesaving Dogs	*61*
7	Dog Detectives	*68*
8	Drug- and Bomb- Detector Dogs	*77*
9	Friend and Companion	*86*
	Index	*93*

Acknowledgments

I wish to extend special thanks to the following people whose unstinting efforts made this book possible: Marcia Koenig of the American Rescue Dog Association; Warren Eckstein of Master Dog Training; Fred Luby, Ron Friend, and Chuck Huthmaker of the U.S. Customs Services; Mr. Ernest Swanton of the Guide Dog Foundation for the Blind; Sgt. Hugh McGowan of the NYCPD Bomb Squad; Cardel Verbruggen; and last, but definitely not least, Lee Hoffman, a very patient and good friend.

I

IN THE BEGINNING

The cavemen had just returned from a successful day of hunting. They usually ate fish, roots, wild fruits, and nuts. Occasionally, when they were lucky, a careless animal would fall into one of the large pits that they had dug. They would kill the trapped animal with rocks and sticks. Sometimes, the cavemen would drive animals over the edge of a cliff to kill them. However, they were not very good hunters and were themselves hunted by other larger and stronger animals.

On this day, they dragged the catch back to their cave. The women and children ran out to see what the men had brought to eat. The animal was cooked inside the cave over a fire. Everyone feasted on the roasted meat, which they did not get often. When they were through, the scraps were carelessly tossed outside the cave entrance.

Later that evening, one of the cavemen heard growling sounds outside. When he went to look, he saw a number of small, furry creatures, which were dogs, fighting over the bones and bits of meat. All of them ran away, except one. The man was curious and so was the dog. They stared at one another for a long time.

The caveman decided to try something. He threw another bone to the dog and waited to see what would happen. The dog fearfully crept closer with his belly dragging along the ground. Suddenly, he grabbed the bone in his mouth and ran off. Each day thereafter, the dog returned to the cave. The man always threw him a scrap. This may have been the way that man and dog began a friendship that has lasted for thousands of years.

Actually, the dog appeared on earth before man. Many people believe that the ancestor of the dog was the wolf. Others disagree. One thing is certain, however—the ancestor of today's dog was at least some sort of wolflike creature.

Man and dog had a lot in common. Men lived in family groups and dogs lived in packs. Both ate meat and moved around from place to place, following the food supply.

At first, man and dog were not friends. Dogs hunted together in packs so that they could catch game that one dog alone could not kill. If other animals attacked the dogs, the pack could drive them away. The dog didn't really need or want a master, and man didn't really want the dog for a friend or companion. They were enemies at first because they competed for the same food.

Sheepdogs drive a flock of sheep in Hawkes Bay, North Island.

Man and dog probably met often in the woods while hunting. After man was through taking the meat he needed, dogs would move in and eat whatever was left behind.

After a while, dogs began to understand that where man was, there was also food. Perhaps dogs began to follow men back to their caves, where more scraps were thrown out.

Having these wild dogs around wasn't bad at all because they would howl when a dangerous animal approached the cave. This was no doubt the first way that dog helped man. Soon, the cavemen threw out even more scraps to keep these protectors around. The dogs ventured closer when they realized that man wasn't going to hurt them.

From that time on, dogs lived most of their lives close to the caves. The female dogs had their litters of puppies near the source of food. One day, some puppies wandered to the front of a cave. The cavemen's children were delighted. They scooped up the furry balls and began playing with them. Later, they took the puppies inside the cave and kept them as pets. This is probably how man and dog first became friends.

When the cavemen went out to hunt, these puppies tagged along and fed on the scraps of the kill. The men noticed that dogs seemed able to sniff the air and find the game easily. This certainly made the hunting business more successful, and a working relationship developed.

When man discovered the bow and arrow, big changes occurred in his relationship with dogs. The bow and arrow would not have been much good if dogs had not been around to find the game. The dogs benefited, too. In return for their

Good sheepdogs will hold sheep motionless with their stares. A national champion shows his skill by holding three strange sheep at the New Zealand Sheepdog Trials at Tai Tapu, South Island.

hunting services, they received food and shelter, plus human companionship which seemed important to them.

Dogs have played an important role in the history of the world. For example, the ancient Egyptians believed that dogs were friends of the gods. They treated them better than they treated many people.

When man finally learned how to grow crops and raise animals for food, hunting was no longer such a necessity.

Hungarian Komondors were first developed over 200 years ago to protect livestock from wolves. This breed is now being used in America against the coyote.

The dog's job changed a bit. Although they still hunted, dogs now guarded their masters' homes, crops, and animal herds.

Today, the farm dog is the handyman of the working dogs. He serves his master in many ways. The farm dog's career is not as exciting as the seeing eye dog or detective dog, but he is just as important. Many a farmer could not do without his hard-working dog.

Some farm dogs are purebreds while others are ordinary mixed breeds. They often sleep in the barn with the horses and eat whatever they can find. They receive little, if any, special training for their job. They just do what comes naturally.

Farm dogs kill rats, weasles, foxes, and other troublesome small animals. They also kill dangerous snakes that find their way into the henhouse to steal eggs. In the past, farm dogs churned the butter and brought water from the well. Today, they still drive the cows to pasture in the morning and then home again at night.

Herding dogs can do the work that one person can never accomplish. They keep the sheep and cattle together. They are able to move them easily from one place to another. They also protect their charges from vicious wolves and human rustlers.

The very special and unique relationship between man and dog has existed since the dawn of time. Over the centuries, we have continued to discover endless ways in which faithful dogs have helped mankind to survive.

2

HUNTING DOGS

It is a crisp, clear November day in upstate New York. The fallen leaves from the trees make a colorful blanket on the ground. A man pulls his car up to the hunting area. His tiny, wire-haired dachshund jumps out of the car. This is a special dachshund. Her name is Clary and her job is to trail and find wounded deer. Earlier in the day, a deer hunter had shot a deer. The animal had been wounded and had run away.

Sometimes, an injured deer can run for miles. It may recover from the wound or linger in pain for days before dying. Good hunters do not want this to happen. That is why Clary is called in to help. Her job is to find the wounded deer, not to hurt it or let the hunter harm it further.

Clary is not a hunting dog. Dachshunds are used to hunt in Germany, but Clary does not hunt. She is on a mission of mercy.

The man attaches a leash to frisky, little Clary. A blaze-orange collar is put around her neck. Blaze orange is a very bright color. It is worn by hunters in the woods so that other hunters do not mistake them for deer. Clary changes immediately from a playful pet to a serious dog. She knows that it is time to go to work.

They go to the spot where the deer was seen last. Clary sniffs all around the area to pick up the deer's scent. Suddenly, she is off. Clary leads her handler deeper and deeper into the woods. They go through swamps and over many hills. Finally, they come upon the wounded deer lying in a bed of tall grass. The handler can tell that the deer is only slightly wounded and will recover. He smiles as the beautiful animal jumps up and bounds away through the woods.

Hunting was one of the very first ways in which dogs served mankind. Man hunted to put food on the table, and it was necessary to have a dog to find the game. Dogs have a strong instinct for the hunt and a keen sense of smell. Hunting is the favorite pastime of many breeds.

Since the Middle Ages (about 476-1492), many different breeds of hunting dogs have been developed. Some dogs are excellent rabbit hunters. Others make better bird dogs. The nobility hunted for sport. The lowly peasants needed dogs to kill rats and other small animals that ate their grain and attacked their chickens.

Terriers of various sorts kill mice or rats that infest buildings. Terriers are also used as hunting dogs by the English, Scottish, Irish, and Welsh. The terrier digs into the ground to go after a fox, badger, weasel, hedgehog, or rat that has

A bird dog waits for his master's command to go to work.

been chased into its burrow or hole. The dog follows the animal's scent. Then, he crawls and digs down through the tunnel until he comes face-to-face with the animal. These brave little dogs will either grab the animal with their teeth or keep it in the hole until their master comes. Today, most terriers are either pets or show dogs.

Fierce hounds are used for hunting wolves, bear, and wild boar. Greyhounds like to chase game. In the woods, hounds track game. When they find it, their masters will kill the animal. Spaniels are used in the swamps because they don't mind getting wet.

When hunters began using guns instead of bows and arrows or spears, new types of hunting dogs were needed. Pointers and setters could show where the game was hidden. Springer spaniels could chase the game from their hiding places in tall grass and under bushes. Retrievers could swim in lakes and rivers and bring back wounded ducks and geese.

In England, large areas of land were cleared in order to make places to use hunting dogs. Soon, the sight of a pack of hounds followed by a group of formally dressed people on horseback became a common sight. They were "riding to the hounds," chasing one poor little fox.

Even the first settlers in America wouldn't think of going into the wilderness without their trusty dogs. On the passenger list of the Mayflower was a mastiff and a spaniel. Hunting dogs went with the pioneers and helped them to shape our nation's history. Without them to help in hunting for food, many pioneers might have starved.

In 1755, Benjamin Franklin had a very unusual idea for using hunting dogs. He thought that dogs should help fight the Indians. Franklin wanted fierce, ferocious dogs to track down the raiding Indians that often scalped the settlers. However, Ben Franklin's idea was never put to the test because people thought it was ridiculous.

Sporting dogs, or gun dogs, help their masters hunt in

Two bird dogs point for their master.

several ways. Pointers, setters, retrievers, and spaniels locate pheasant, partridge, or quail by following their windborne scent. Pointers actually point to the birds when they find them. When a dog points, he stands still and faces in the direction of the birds.

Spaniels and retrievers flush, or chase, the birds from their hiding places in tall grass. When the frightened birds fly up in the air, the hunter shoots them. After the gun is fired, a retriever looks to see where the bird lands. Then, he proudly brings it back to his master.

When a retriever finds the bird, he takes it very carefully in his mouth. He does not damage the game bird in any way.

Pointing to birds hidden in the tall grass.

Some retrievers, like the Labrador, are excellent swimmers and can bring the fallen bird out of the water. This is partly due to their heritage. Many years ago, these dogs worked with fishermen in Newfoundland, which is an island off of the eastern coast of Canada. The dogs swam in the dangerous northern waters where their job was to bring the fish nets up to the side of the fishing boats.

Setters find birds in a slightly different way. A setter runs back and forth across the fields until he smells the birds' scent. Then, he points to where they can be located. Hopefully, the birds are too busy eating and pecking at the ground to notice the dog. The setter waits until his master commands him to move. Slowly, the dog creeps up on the unsuspecting birds. As soon as the birds hear the dog, they fly up into the air. The hunter shoots. The dog is praised for his good work. There are three breeds of setters — the English, the Gordon, and the Irish.

Probably the best all-purpose hunting dog is the German short-haired pointer. He is good at hunting ducks as well as pheasant, quail, partridge, and even rabbits, raccoons, and possums. The pointer's keen sense of smell enables him to find the game and retrieve the birds whether they fall on land or in the water.

Sporting dogs are never gun shy. The sound of a gun being fired does not frighten them. In fact, to these dogs, the sound of the shot is a signal to go, find, and fetch the bird.

Hounds are also excellent hunting dogs. They use either their eyes to follow the game or their noses to pick up the scent. There are hounds that hunt for foxes with their masters. These are called foxhounds. The foxhound is trained to follow the fox's scent. When he finds it, he will give "voice" or bark. When the fox is cornered and unable to get away, the hounds begin barking again.

Foxhounds often hunt in packs of fifteen or more dogs. They are trained to work together and usually live in the same kennels. Foxhounds originally hunted in packs for wild boar, deer, and wolves. As these animals became scarce, the fox became the object of the hunt.

Today, in some northern states, the hunters kill the fox. In southern states, the fox is usually allowed to go free. In the west, these dogs sometimes hunt coyotes instead of foxes.

Coonhounds are dogs that hunt raccoons. Raccoons like to live in swamps, thick forests, and near streams or ponds. They are nocturnal animals that sleep in trees during the day and prowl for food at night. The coonhounds, therefore, must hunt at night. When they pick up the scent of the raccoon, they begin to "bay." The dog makes a deep, throaty howl which sounds very different from a bark. The coonhounds follow the scent trail until they find the raccoon. The raccoon usually tries to escape by running up a tree. The coonhounds bay and make a lot of noise at the base of the tree until their masters come.

Other types of hounds hunt by sight rather than by scent. These are called gazehounds. Some types of gazehounds are greyhounds, Afghan hounds, and whippets. Today, these dogs are used for racing because of their incredible speed.

The whippets, usually six at a time, race after a "lure." The lure can be anything from a rabbit skin to some rags tied to the end of a long string. The lure is reeled in by a mechanical device and bounces along the ground. It really looks like a running rabbit to the dogs. All the dogs are released at the same time to chase the lure, and the first dog over the finish line wins the race.

Today, more dogs are kept for hunting than for any other purpose. Although this was the first way that dogs helped man, it was far from the last.

3

SLED DOGS

One of the most famous sled dogs was Balto, a Siberian husky. In 1925, a very dangerous diphtheria epidemic threatened the people of Nome, Alaska. A special medicine was needed to save them. It was far away in Anchorage. To make matters worse, there was a terrible blizzard. Airplanes in those days could not make this dangerous journey. The only way to bring the medicine to Nome was by dog sled.

A plan was formed. Nineteen sled drivers and their dog teams living at different points along the way set up a chain. The medicine was passed from one dog sled team to the next almost as if they were in a relay race. They crossed treacherous mountains covered with deep snow. The sure-footed sled dogs crossed moving ice floes in the dark. The men, their dogs, and even the medicine were always in danger of freezing, but the brave dogs ran on. Finally, there were only fifty miles to go. The lead dog of the last dog team was named Balto. Through temperatures of forty degrees below zero, Balto showed the way to his driver and to the rest of the dog team. Balto's courage was honored when his statue was placed in New York City's Central Park.

The very first dogs that were used to pull a sled were any kind that the Eskimos could find to do the work. These early sled dogs were a mixture of many different breeds. They may even have been related to wolves. They were mostly dogs that stayed around the camps and were used for hunting.

The lives of these sled dogs were not easy. They slept outside in the frigid temperatures even during blizzards. They ate whatever bits of frozen fish were thrown to them. If they were thirsty, they ate snow. In warm weather, they were turned loose to find whatever food they could. These dogs were half-starved much of the time. They fought among themselves for any scraps that came their way and became mean.

Today, some people think that all sled dogs are vicious, but this is not true. As men learned to take better care of their animals, they discovered how gentle, brave, and helpful these hardy workers could be.

The Eskimos kept those dogs that worked the hardest and were the strongest. They were bred with other good sled dogs. Soon, better sled dogs were being used by the Eskimos.

The three kinds of dogs that make the best sled-pullers are

the Siberian husky, Russian Samoyed, and Alaskan malamute. All three are very strong and can tolerate the cold weather in which they must live and work.

The Siberian husky was used for centuries by the Chuchis people of northeastern Siberia in Russia. He not only pulled the sleds, but was the family pet. The Siberian husky was so important to these people that he was allowed to sleep inside with the family a night. Today, he is a friendly dog and companion as a result of this kind treatment.

The thick, double coat of the Siberian husky is important so that he can endure the cold weather where he lives. The undercoat is soft and the top coat is long. His fur can be silvery gray, black with white markings, or a light brown color. The intelligent eyes are brown or bright sky blue. Sometimes, these dogs have one eye of each color. Many people think his face resembles that of a fox.

Like other sled dogs, he has a "snowshoe foot." His feet are slightly webbed between the toes. This helps him move more easily through the snow. Although the Siberian husky is smaller than the other two types of sled dogs, he is the fastest. He is also quite strong and good at following trails.

The Siberian husky first appeared in Alaska in 1909. At this time, a Russian trader entered his team of smaller, foxlike Siberian huskies in the famous All Alaska Sweepstakes. This is the biggest dog-racing contest in Alaska. The race went from Nome, Alaska, to Candle, Alaska. To everyone's surprise, the Siberian husky team came in third. From that time on, huskies competed in nearly all of the dog races, and did very well.

Another type of sled dog is the Russian Samoyed. He was found living with a small tribe of people called the Samoyed, for whom he is named. These people live in northern Siberia, above the Arctic Circle. The Samoyed dog could herd reindeer, hunt, pull sleds, and be a wonderful companion for these isolated people.

The Samoyed is a beautiful dog. His color is white or a creamy off-white. Like the husky, he has two coats of fur to keep him warm. The undercoat is thick, soft, and woolly. The beautiful outercoat is so long and shiny that the Samoyed people used to weave it into yarn when the dog shed in warmer weather. The Samoyed's face is special because he always looks as though he is smiling. The lips of his mouth turn up at the corners and he looks every bit the friendly fellow that he is.

The last type of sled dog is the Alaskan malamute, one of the oldest sled dog breeds in existence. He was discovered living among the Malamute Eskimos who lived along the shores of Kotzebue Sound in northwestern Alaska. The Malamute Eskimos did not permit their dogs to be mated with any other breed. They valued their sled dogs very highly and treated them kindly. The malamute today is a friendly and affectionate dog.

The malamute also has a double coat of fur with a handsome ruff around his neck and shoulders. The undercoat can be two inches thick. It is woolly and oily to help him stay dry in the snow. The outer hair is very long and rough. He can be light gray or black with white markings. He is very powerfully built and can weigh as much as eighty-five pounds.

A sled dog carries equipment for the Larsen Expedition.

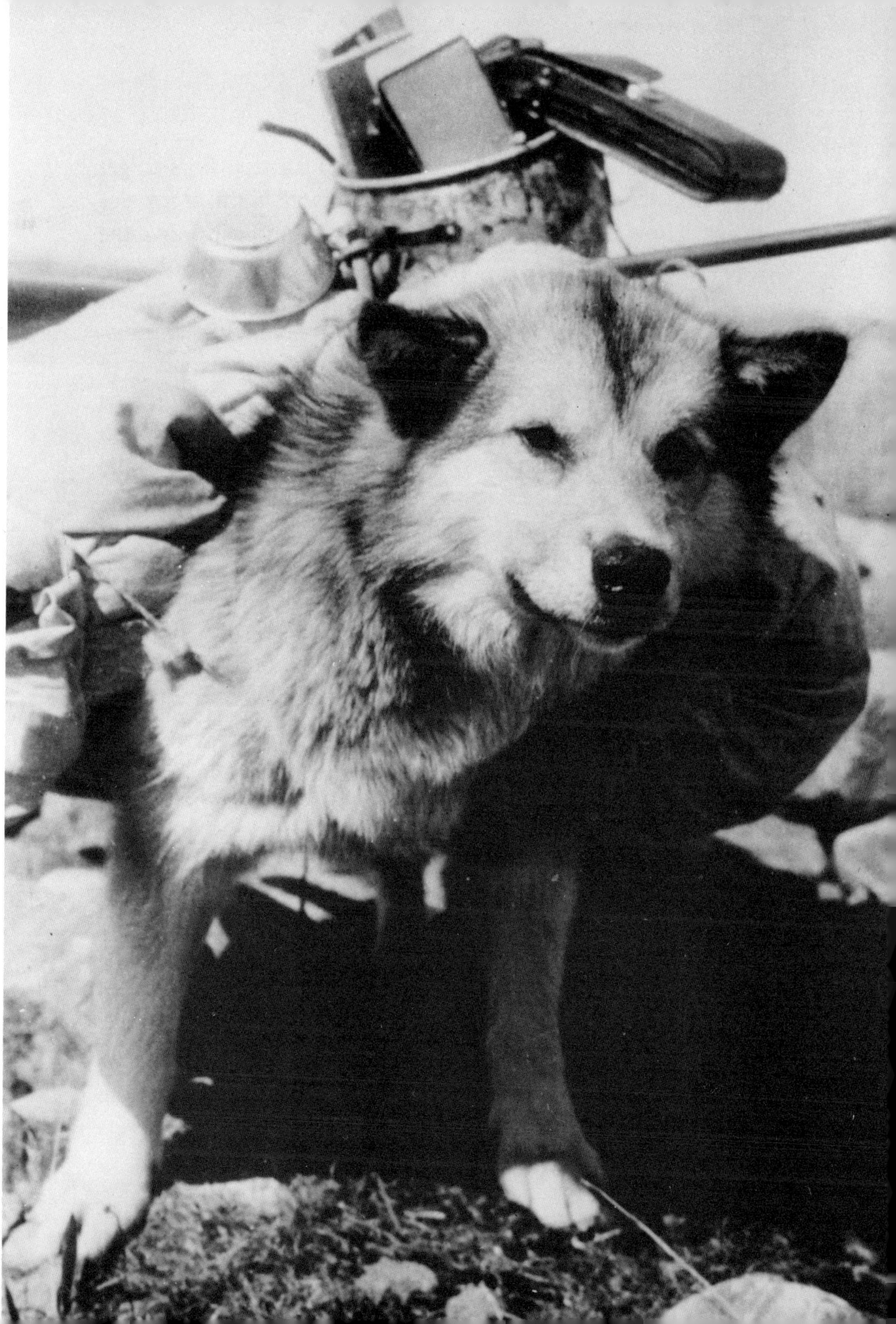

Even today, when there is little need for dog sleds to get from place to place, the Alaskan malamute is still a popular dog. He is the strongest type of sled dog and can move the heaviest loads.

Other than the sled itself, the sled dogs were an Eskimo's most valuable treasures. They were his only means of transportation over the ice and through the deep snow. Even in summer, they were put to work towing boats along the shore. The sled dogs could also pull any kind of heavy load through mud and slush for hundreds of miles. To do this, the Eskimos used sledges. A sledge is similar to a sled except that it has runners. Therefore, the load the dog was pulling would not tip over. A sled rides higher about a foot and a half above the snow.

One sled-dog owner used his dogs during the Klondike Gold Rush in the 1890s. This dog team hauled the prospector's belongings to the Yukon in northwestern Canada and made a great deal of money for their owner. Sled-dog teams have also been used to carry the mail. One mailman in Canada delivered his load of mail by dog team for thirty-five years.

When airplanes began to cross the North and South Poles, sled dogs were still useful. They accompanied many explorers on their expeditions. Sled dogs went with Robert Peary, the famous explorer, when he discovered the North Pole. A team of Siberian huskies went on an expedition to Antarctica with Admiral Byrd in 1951.

Today, sled-dog racing has become a popular sport. However, the sport is not new. It began in Alaska where the

The fastest dog team in the Klondyke.

highest prize money was paid to the winners. The sport then spread to Greenland, Labrador, Canada, and the United States. The sled dogs love to race. To them it is more than just hard work — it is fun.

A good sled dog wants to run. He has a strong desire to pull any load and to please his master. The dogs must learn to follow certain commands. The driver shouts to his dogs as they gallop along a snowy trail at a fast pace. The commands are: Mush, Go, Stop, Gee (turn right), Haw (turn left), and Whoa.

Usually, there are nine dogs on a team, but there can be as many as fourteen or as few as five. The number of dogs needed depends on the size of the load the dog team must pull. Some sledges can have as many as seventeen dogs on a team. In good weather, a dog team can travel at about twelve to fourteen miles per hour. The dogs are harnessed or connected, but the driver does not pull on the reins. Instead, the dogs simply do what he commands them to do.

The most important dog on the team is the lead dog. He has a very special task — to decide which way the team will go. When he hears his master's voice commanding "Gee!", the lead dog is responsible for seeing that all of the other dogs follow him. The lead dog is also the one who must know when to go around obstacles in the dog team's path. Most important, he is the one who finds his way home in a snowstorm when it is impossible to see very far ahead.

The sled dogs are among the hardest-working dogs that have helped mankind.

4

SEEING-EYE AND HEARING-EAR DOGS

Molly hugs the large, yellow dog for the last time, then waves goodbye. Big tears roll down her cheeks as the Labrador retriever climbs into the back of a van. The dog's name is Ingrid. She has lived with Molly's family since she was just a small ball of yellow fur, only six weeks old. Now Ingrid is one year old and fully grown. Today, she is going to a new home — a school for special dogs. Ingrid will train to be a guide dog.

When Ingrid's difficult training is through, she will serve as a pair of eyes for her blind master or mistress. Molly is very sad to see Ingrid leave. However, she is also proud of the part she has played in training Ingrid.

The idea of using dogs to help blind people began in Germany. After World War I, there were many soldiers who had been blinded during the fighting. Dogs were trained to help these men live a nearly normal life. The dogs would guide the men through the streets and around any obstacles that stood in their way.

In 1927, a blind American man named Morris S. Frank heard of a magazine article about these specially trained dogs. The article was written by Mrs. Dorothy H. Eustis. Mr. Frank wrote to Mrs. Eustis, and she invited him to visit her in Switzerland. Mrs. Eustis said she would train a guide dog for him, but he would first have to learn how to handle it.

Mrs. Eustis started her own guide dog school in Switzerland. The school was named Fortunate Fields. It was located next to a beautiful, large park. At Fortunate Fields, there were sidewalks, curbs, steps, and many other obstacles such as telephone poles and ditches. These are the very things a blind person might find every day when walking down the street.

After several months of training, Mr. Frank returned to America with Buddy, his German shepherd guide dog. Even though there was more traffic and noise in America, Buddy did his job well. As a result of this meeting of Mr. Frank and Buddy, the first school known as The Seeing Eye was started in Nashville, Tennessee in 1929.

Today, there are several organizations that train dogs for the blind. They are Guiding Eyes, The Seeing Eye, Pilot Dog, Leader Dog, Second Sight, and Guide Dogs for the Blind. These dogs are given free to blind people who really need them. With guide dogs by their sides, blind people can do many things that they couldn't manage before. They can

Guide dog and mistress practice on an obstacle course.

visit friends, go shopping, attend school, and much more. They can do all of these things safely with the help of their special dogs.

Certain breeds make the best guide dogs. They are Labrador retrievers, German shepherds, golden retrievers, collies, and boxers. The most important qualifications for a guide dog are that he is friendly, calm, and under control at all times. He must not be shy with people, children, or cars. Automobile horns and other loud noises should not scare him or make him nervous. A guide dog must be intelligent and want to please his master. He must also be healthy and measure about twenty-two inches high at his shoulder.

The size of a guide dog is important. Since a guide dog walks by his master's side, the person can feel the dog's movement as he stops, turns, or pauses. A person could not do this with a very small dog, and a very large dog might be too difficult for a blind person to handle.

Recently, the Guide Dog Foundation for the Blind in Smithtown, New York, developed a completely new breed of dog. It is called a golden Lab. The golden Lab makes the very best guide dog of all. This new breed is half golden retriever and half Labrador retriever. He combines the wonderful temperament of the golden retriever with the toughness of the Labrador retriever. The golden Lab also makes a first-class city guide dog.

When guide dog puppies are about six weeks old, they are sent to live with foster families. It is much better for these puppies to grow up with a loving boy or girl than to be raised in a kennel. In kennels, they risk catching certain infections. Besides, living with a child early in life helps the guide dogs learn how to get along with people. The children are also able to teach the puppies basic obedience. The dogs are taken to stores and other crowded places to get accustomed to many people and loud noises.

The special training at the school takes from three to six months. Obedience is the first lesson a guide dog learns. He must sit, stay, and follow other important commands. A stiff, U-shaped harness is then placed on the dog. When the harness goes on, the dog knows it is time to work.

A guide dog quickly becomes accustomed to city noises. He is taught to stop for any hazards such as clotheslines, low-hanging branches, and cars. He learns to stop at every

A guide dog leads his master down a flight of steep stairs.

corner until his master commands him to go forward. The hardest lesson the dog must learn is to decide for himself if it is safe for his master to cross the street.

The guide dog can perform many other tasks. He can pick up objects such as keys that his master drops. He is able to lead his master to doors. At the end of the training period, the trainer may put a blindfold on himself and take the dog out into the world. This is the guide dog's final test to see if he can be trusted to care for a human life.

If the dog has learned his lessons well, he is then paired with a blind person. For the next four weeks, the dog and his new master learn to work together as a team. The owner first learns to care for and handle his new friend. During this time, they actually live together at a special training center. The blind person is taught to understand what his dog tries to tell him. The most important thing the blind person learns is to trust his guide dog. By the time the man and dog team graduate from the training program, they are also the best of friends. The total cost of this training is about $4,000.

Guide dogs are indeed special dogs for special people. One of the most special guide dogs of all is Max, a yellow Labrador retriever. While Max was still living with his foster family, he was hit by a car. Max's left front leg was so badly injured that it had to be removed by the doctors. Within weeks, Max was back on his three good legs, doing everything he had done before the accident. Word of Max's ability reached Mr. Ernest Swanton of the Guide Dog Foundation for the Blind in Smithtown, New York. Today, Max has a permanent home there.

Three affectionate and loyal guide dogs pose with a blind girl.

Dogs are now helping deaf people as well. A hearing-ear dog is specially trained to be his master's ears. He can respond to the sounds of telephones, doorbells, alarm clocks, car horns, babies' cries, smoke alarms, and much more.

Unlike guide dogs, hearing-ear dogs notice all of the sounds around them. Many dogs that do not make good guide dogs often make excellent hearing-ear dogs.

In 1976, the American Humane Association of Denver, Colorado, first began training dogs for the deaf. They found that any kind of dog could be used, even mixed breeds or mutts. Small to medium-sized dogs worked best and were easiest to handle.

When the trainers select a dog, they look for a friendly animal that likes people. The dog must also be healthy, intelligent, and not mind wearing a leash. Many of these animals are found in dog pounds or are strays found on the street. It is a wonderful way to give unwanted dogs a new chance for a useful life.

The dog is given a two-week obedience course either right away or later on in the program. Hearing-ear dogs then get special auditory-awareness training. During this time, the trainer runs with the dog to the source of a sound. This is done over and over again. Soon, the hearing-ear dog understands that there is something special about sounds. Then, he is taught to move back and forth between the trainer and the sound. If the doorbell rings, the dog moves from the door to his owner to let him know he has a visitor. Sometimes, a treat may be used to lure the dog to the door when the bell rings. The training takes about twenty minutes a day.

The dog behaves the same way when the telephone rings.

Although deaf people can't use a telephone in the usual manner, they have a special teletype machine that is attached to the phone. This machine writes down what the person at the other end of the phone says.

The dog is trained to alert his master to an alarm clock or smoke alarm. Since people are usually asleep when these sounds are heard, the dog must either jump up on the bed to wake him up or lick his face. This training takes about two to four months. If the dog is ready, he is paired with his new deaf master. Together, they will learn to work as a team.

Unfortunately, there are many more people who want hearing-ear dogs than there are dogs. That is why the deaf person who lives alone, and needs help most, usually gets a dog first.

A law recently passed in New York State gives hearing-ear dogs the same rights as guide dogs. Now, a hearing-ear dog can go on buses, trains, planes, and any other kind of public transportation with his master. He is allowed into public buildings, such as stores, where other dogs are not welcome.

Almost every handicapped person can be helped by a trained dog for a friend and companion. For a person confined to a wheelchair, a dog can be trained to turn on the TV, fetch the newspaper, get mail out of the mailbox, and much more. A dog can learn to do just about everything for a handicapped person.

Dogs have even been trained to help people with a disease called epilepsy. When an epileptic person is about to have a seizure, the dog will sense it. He will pull a special alarm cord in the person's home that calls for help. If the person is unconscious and away from home, the dog wears a special tag around his neck with information about his master's disease. The faithful dog will stand over his master, guarding him until help comes.

Loving, intelligent, and loyal dogs of all breeds make it possible for blind, deaf, and handicapped people to live fuller lives. No longer must they depend on other people for everything. With the help of their dogs, these people can now manage well on their own.

5

SEARCH AND RESCUE DOGS

Many years ago, a mountain climber in the Swiss Alps was struggling through the deep snow. Suddenly, he heard a frightening, rumbling sound. At first, the sound was far away, but the sound grew louder and louder. Then, he realized what was happening. Avalanche! It was too late for the mountaineer to escape. Soon, it seemed as though the whole mountain of snow slid down upon him. Only his face was left uncovered by the icy coldness.

The man was injured and could not get up. He cried out for help, but no one heard him. Long into the night, he waited for help to come. When he had almost given up hope, he heard the barking of dogs as they bounded through the powdery snow. The dogs were upon him before he knew it.

Four huge dogs began to lick his face in a very friendly manner. The mountaineer knew that he was saved. These

Edi Rodel with an eight-week-old St. Bernard pup.

were the famous St. Bernard dogs. They were kept by the monks who ran a hospice, or inn, in the Great St. Bernard Pass between France and Italy.

Two of the giant, brown-and-white dogs laid down beside the man. He could feel their soft, furry bodies begin to warm his nearly frozen bones. The other two dogs galloped off to go for human help. Meanwhile, the two remaining dogs kept licking his cold face to keep him awake. If the man fell asleep in the snow, he might freeze to death.

For more than 300 years, the St. Bernard dogs rescued many people from a snowy death. Although these dogs are usually shown on television with a small keg of brandy tied beneath their chins, this is just a colorful story and not the truth. The dogs patrolled in a foursome after snowstorms to look for lost travelers. Two dogs always kept the victim warm with their bodies while the other two went for help. This was an easy task for the gentle giants. A St. Bernard can weigh as much as a man — 160 to 200 pounds.

The dogs were first brought to the hospice between 1660 and 1670. Because they were so gentle and affectionate, they made wonderful friends and companions for the monks. It was very lonely during the long winters when the snow was too deep for visitors to get there.

There were always a few people who tried to travel the mountain pass. The monks would rescue travelers that were stranded. Soon, they were taking their large, friendly dogs with them. The monks discovered that their St. Bernards had a keen sense of smell. Because of this, the dogs were better at finding people than the monks were. The dogs could even find people who were completely buried under many feet of snow. Before long, the monks and the St. Bernards began to work together in their rescue work.

The dogs seemed to have a rescue instinct. Young St. Bernards were taken along on snow patrols with older, more experienced dogs. In this way, the young dogs watched the older dogs at work. Soon, they knew what they were supposed to do.

A keen sense of smell is not the only talent of these special dogs. Many people say that they can tell when an avalanche or "white death" is about to happen. St. Bernard dogs have been known to run away from a particular area just before a mountain of snow came crashing down on the spot where they had been standing.

During the past 300 years, these powerful animals have saved at least 2,000 lives. St. Bernard dogs continue to live at the hospice even today. Sometimes, they work as guide dogs in the Alps. They locate trails through the snow for the people following them.

There is not much rescue work going on anymore. Very few people try to walk through this dangerous area. They prefer safer ways of modern travel such as trains or planes.

One of the most famous St. Bernards of all time was Barry. Barry saved at least forty lives between 1800 and 1810. There is a story that the forty-first, thinking Barry was a bear, shot him. This is untrue. Barry actually died of old age in his bed.

At the St. Bernard Hospice in the Swiss Alps today, a monk poses with a few St. Bernard puppies.

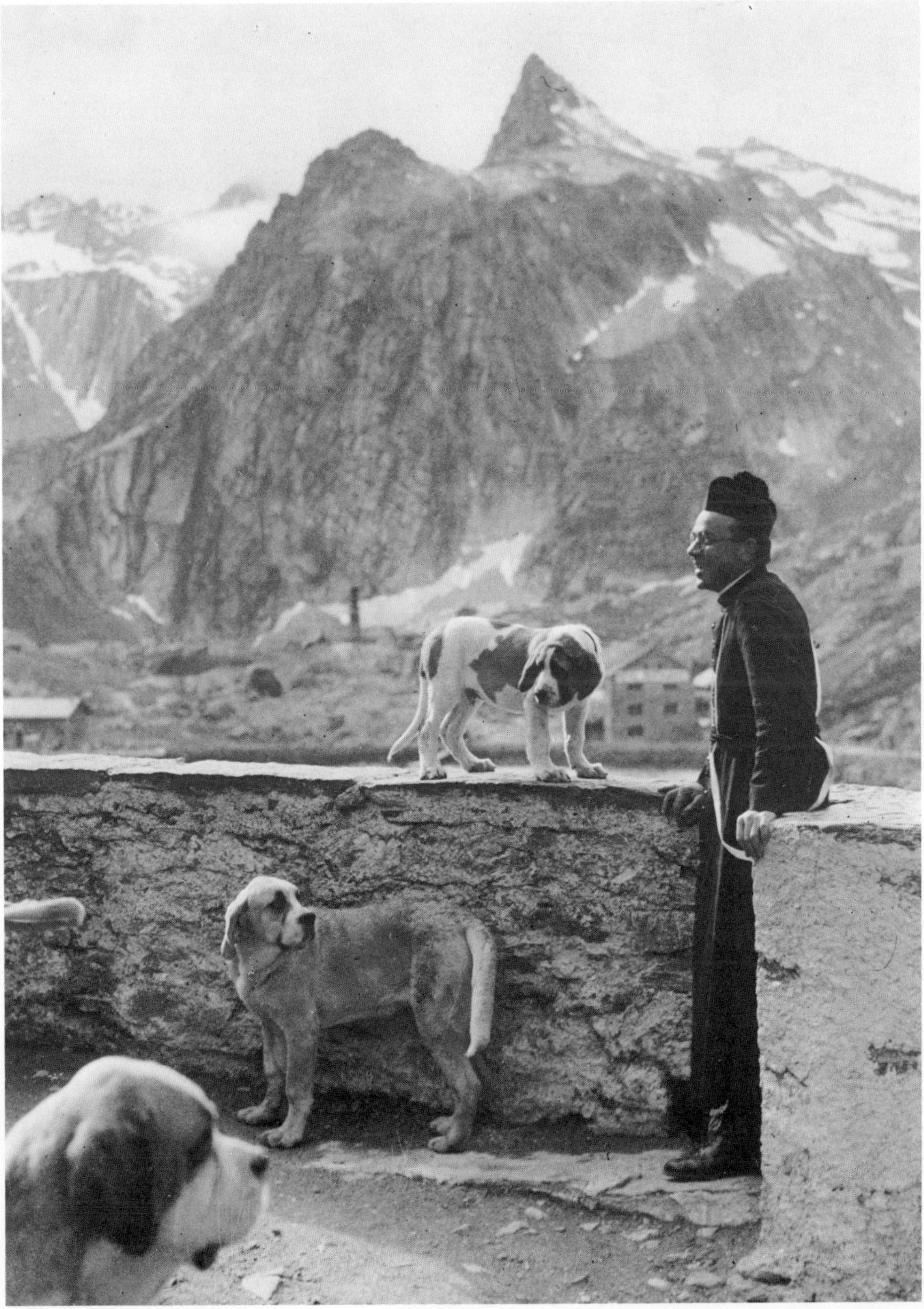

Barry 1799–1814

Während Jahren war dieser unvergleichliche Bernhardiner für viele Wanderer und Kaufleute auf dem beschwerlichen Weg über den Grossen St. Bernhard ein sicherer Wegweiser und Helfer. Er rettete 40 Menschenleben aus Eis und Schnee. Mit 12 Jahren brachte der Prior des Kloster-Hospizes den weltberühmt gewordenen Hund nach Bern in gute Pflege, wo er 1814 starb. Noch heute, nach über 150 Jahren, ist sein Name unvergessen.

Präparat aus dem Berner Naturhistorischen Museum

The famous Barry located more missing travelers than any other St. Bernard.

Today, in modern Switzerland, the army rescue service discovered that other kinds of dogs can qualify for rescue work. They now use German shepherds also. The shepherds are trained to locate their masters who have hidden themselves in the snow. After a while, the dogs understand that they are supposed to find any buried person. Some of these dogs are so good at their job, they can tell whether the person beneath the snow is dead or alive.

There is yet another kind of lifesaving dog. He is called the search and rescue dog. These dogs are air scenters. They can detect the scent that every human being gives off into the air. If a person has been missing several days, the scent trail on the ground is gone. But the person, dead or alive, is still giving off a scent.

The American Rescue Dog Association located in Seattle, Washington, believes that German shepherds are the best type of dog for this work. They are large in size, very strong, and love their work. Once these specially trained dogs have found the air scent, they follow their noses until they find the person they are looking for.

A search and rescue puppy starts his training when he is six weeks old. The first thing he must learn is socialization — getting the puppy used to the sights, sounds, and smells of our world. He must not be frightened by any of these things. Puppies are taken for car rides and must stay alone in the car for a time. They go for walks in the woods and learn to swim. They use stairs and walk on many different surfaces such as wood, concrete, or tile. The puppy gets accustomed to the loud noises of a vacuum cleaner, lawn mower, and car, among others.

At work in the Swiss Alps.

A rescue dog uncovers his buried trainer in a test of his ability.

A rescue dog in the Swiss Alps locates someone that is buried under several feet of snow.

The puppy then plays the "Runaway Game." This is like playing hide-and-seek. The owner hides and the puppy must find him. This game prepares the dog for the day when he will have to find lost people.

Finally, the day comes when the handler tells the dog to "Find." The dog learns that this means he is to find a person. Special training is also given for avalanche work. The handler uses a different command such as "Seek," when he wants the dog to look for people buried beneath many feet of snow. The different command word tells the dog he is searching for something he cannot see.

When the American Rescue Dog Association receives a call for help, they must first decide a few important matters. Where is the area to be searched? How large is it? Who will

Racing in the direction of a scent, this dog is on the trail.

cover which part of the area? When these questions have been answered, each handler will divide his area into four parts or quarters. The team of one dog and one handler will search one quarter at a time before moving on to the next. The dog runs ahead of the handler, sniffing and searching all the while.

The dogs locate the air scent of a person by investigating. They move back and forth in front of their handler. The dog is always looking for the scent. He knows it is somewhere. He alone must find and follow it.

When the dog finally picks up the scent, he follows it until he finds what he is looking for. When the dog is successful, he is rewarded with plenty of love and praise. When he is rewarded for a job well done, it makes him want to do good jobs over and over again.

The dogs are able to smell a human scent up to two miles away, through twenty-five feet of snow or two feet of dirt or rubble. That is why these dogs are so valuable when looking for someone lost in the wilderness. They are also called in to find people after disasters such as tornadoes, plane crashes, floods, and earthquakes have occured. Recently, search and rescue dogs were called in to search for survivors when Mount St. Helens, a volcano in Washington State, erupted.

The training of a search and rescue dog takes about one year. The handler must also go to school because he and his German shepherd will work as a team. The dog and the handler work together for about ten hours a week. Not only do they learn their jobs, but they become the best of friends. The dog learns to obey his owner's commands. The owner

A dog handler assigns a search area to another dog team.

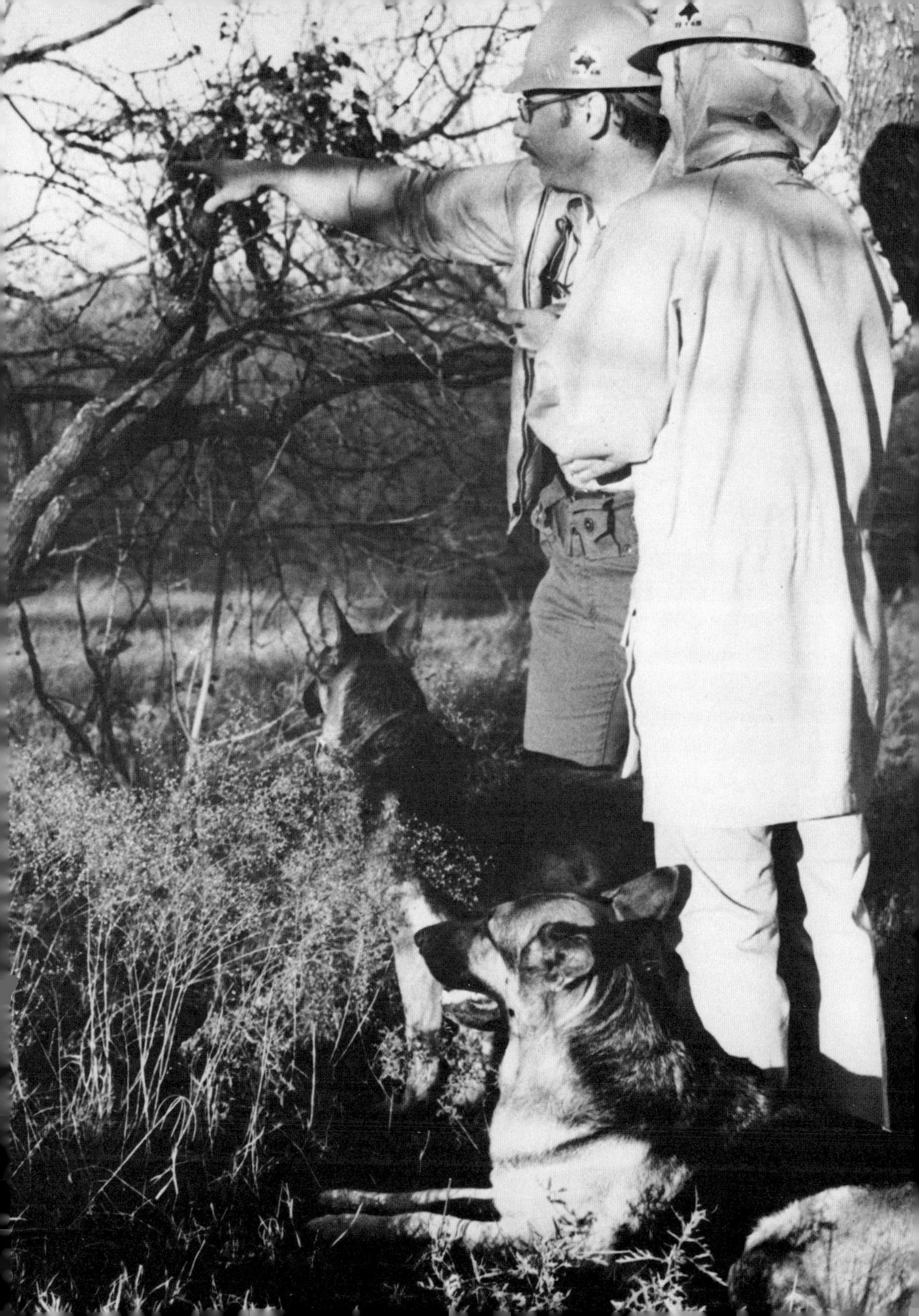

Dog and handler search ruins for tornado victims in Wichita Falls, Texas.

A rescue team prepares for a search in Idaho.

Handler and dog ride in a helicopter on the way to a search.

learns to understand his dog's signal. The dog signals his handler in a special way when he has found a lost or injured person. Each dog signals differently. Some sit, others may begin to dig.

The handler must also learn first aid so that he can help an injured person once he has been found. He or she must be in top physical condition and know how to survive in the wilderness, since actual searches can last a long time and be extremely dangerous.

When a search and rescue dog team arrives at the scene of a search, they are ready to stay for five days if necessary. Each team will search from morning until night. They sometimes spend the night in the wilderness and start early again the next morning. The handler carries food, first-aid supplies and a two-way radio to keep in touch with other search and rescue teams.

Many lost hunters or children are alive today because of the efforts of these brave dogs. They are tremendously grateful that such dogs were so willing to help them in their time of need.

6

LIFESAVING DOGS

The little boy swims out in the lake. There are no lifeguards on duty. The child thinks he is a better swimmer than he really is. Suddenly, he gets a painful cramp in his leg. The boy becomes frightened and starts splashing about. He can't swim back to the beach and he can't stay afloat for long, either.

The boy shouts for help, as he can barely keep his head above water. Other people on the beach look up. On the shore sits a big, black dog with long, silky fur. He is at the beach with his master. The dog's large square head comes up when he hears the child's screams. In an instant, the dog jumps up and runs into the water. With long, sure strokes, he swims quickly toward the boy.

People on the beach see only the dog's big black head moving through the water. Just before he reaches the boy, the dog circles around in front of him. His head is facing toward the beach. The dog turns to look at the child, as if to say, "Grab me!" The boy somehow understands. He grabs onto the dog's fur, near the tail. The black dog slowly tows the frightened child back to the shore and to safety. This brave and courageous lifesaver is a Newfoundland. It is a breed of dog with a proud history of water-rescue work.

No one knows exactly where the breed originated. Some say the Basque fishermen brought their great Pyrenees dogs with them in the 1600s to Newfoundland from the Pyrenees mountains of Spain and France. Then, they supposedly crossed them with Labrador retrievers. Others believe that the great Pyrenees dogs were crossed with the black St. John's Newfoundland dog. No one knows which story is true.

Many of the early Newfoundlands, or "Newfs," were black and white. Some were taken back to England on trading ships. The breed was improved and perfected there. Later, Newfs became very popular in Europe, Canada, and the United States.

Nature made the Newfoundland a perfect water lifesaving dog. He is big, strong, and sturdy. He is also gentle and loving with people. The Newfoundland is so powerful a swimmer that he can easily save a drowning man and pull him to shore. This is because his strong back legs enable him to swim long distances. The Newfoundland never paddles like most dogs. He does a breast stroke that moves him through the water more like a seal than a dog. His feet move in long, curved strokes.

He also has big, webbed front feet with skin that is

stretched between the toes. He has two coats of hair. The top coat is straight and rough. The undercoat is soft and very thick. The fur is oily — this helps keep the icy water away from the dog's skin.

The color of his fur is usually black. Sometimes, the fur has a tint of chocolate brown. Newfs can also be white with black markings. A dog with fur this color is called a Landseer. He is named after a famous artist. In 1800, Sir Edwin Landseer painted several famous pictures of these black-and-white dogs.

The Newfoundland is an expert watchdog and babysitter. In Newfoundland, these dogs are often used to pull small carts, piled high with heavy loads. They played a major part in helping to develop the island of Newfoundland which is located off of the eastern shore of Canada.

These giant dogs helped the island's fishermen pull in their heavy fishing nets. They could also dive for fish. As the fishing industry grew, sailors became aware of the dog's swimming ability. The Newfoundlands were soon taken on larger, commercial ships. They rescued sailors who were swept overboard in stormy seas. They also carried the ships' towlines ashore in their strong teeth. The Newfoundland was always ready to rescue men and equipment that had fallen overboard.

There are many stories about how Newfs have rescued people. They pulled them out of the dykes, or water-filled ditches, in Holland, from the ocean off of Canada, and from beaches in North America and Europe. Some Newfs have even rescued other dogs.

It is believed that early Newfs were used by the ancient

Romans. In a museum in Naples, Italy, there is an old statue which dates back to the Roman days. The statue shows two large Newf-like dogs saving drowning people from the sea.

A Newfoundland is buried on the grounds of Windsor Castle in England because he rescued a drowning man. There is a story that a Newfoundland saved Napoleon's life when he fell out of a boat one dark, stormy night.

In 1807, an English ship was sinking off of the coast of Maryland. Another ship named the *Canton* came along. With the aid of the English ship's two Newfoundlands, the crew of the sinking ship was pulled to safety. The English sailors were so grateful that they gave the Newfoundlands to the American sailors on the *Canton*. In time, these two dogs were bred with American retrievers. The result is the dog known today as the Chesapeake Bay retriever.

In 1919, a Newf named Tang rescued ninety-two people from a sinking ship by carrying a rope through water too rough for lifeboats. The rope was then used to tow the disabled boat to shore.

In Brittany, France, the dogs work in teams. They are taught to flip a drowning person over onto his back. Then, one Newf grabs the person's shoulder or upper arm gently with his teeth and pulls him ashore. In Australia, they work as lifeguards' assistants on many beaches.

People in the United States are also trying to use these dogs as lifesavers. About seven years ago, the Newfoundland Club of America started water tests for these brave dogs. The club wanted to keep the breed's talent for water rescue from being lost. The water tests are divided into a

This Newfoundland dog jumps into the water to rescue his trainer and tow him to shore.

A man being towed in by Kivi, a well-trained lifesaver.

junior division and a senior division. They combine obedience training with tests of the dog's natural instinct for water rescue.

Instinct is something that the dog does naturally. A Newfoundland will simply jump into the water and splash playfully about. He never needs to take a swimming lesson. When the dog's instinct is combined with training, the Newfoundland becomes an expert lifesaver.

To win a junior certificate, the Newfoundland must pass several tests. He must retrieve objects from the water and tow a boat for fifty to seventy-five feet in shallow water. He must deliver a line across fifty feet of water. The Newfoundland must have very strong teeth for his work. If he passes all these tests, he wins the title of Water Dog.

For the senior certificate, he must pass several more difficult tests. The biggest test comes when the dog's handler falls overboard into the water on purpose. The Newfoundland must jump into the water and drag his handler ashore. He must also tow a boat to shore by taking a life ring attached to a rope out to the boat. Another senior test requires the dog to retrieve an object that is under one and one-half to two feet of water. If the Newf passes these tests, he wins the title of Water Rescue Dog. If he fails any one of these tests, he fails the entire test. Water-rescue training can be done in three to four months, but it usually takes longer.

Today, a third division of water tests is being prepared. In these tests, the dog must show that he will not harm the person he is rescuing. He must also be able to handle a drowning person who is so frightened that he could fight and pull the dog underwater, too.

This dog holds a bumper with a short length of line attached, swims out to a stranded boat, and tows it to shore.

Newfs are now being trained to let the drowning person grab onto the fur on their back, just above their tails. A person should never grab the Newf's long tail. The dog needs to use his tail as a rudder to help him change direction if necessary.

In the future, it may become common to see a big, long-haired black dog standing on a beach alongside the lifeguard. It will mean double protection for swimmers. As a result, there will be fewer water accidents. No other dog is as strong or has rescued as many people as the Newfoundland.

7

DOG DETECTIVES

On June 9, 1977, almost 200 state and local police, prison guards, FBI agents, and helicopters searched a wide area around the Brushy Mountain State Prison in Tennessee. The prison bloodhound team was also called into action to do what they do best—track people. They were looking for James Earl Ray—the convicted killer of Martin Luther King. Five other prisoners also escaped and ran off into the heavily wooded mountains.

For thirty-six hours, the bloodhounds sniffed their way across a river, up a hill, through underbrush, and into another wooded area. They worked in teams of one man and one dog.

At first, they worked in relays, taking turns tracking. The dogs kept searching for a scent, but could find none. They became confused. The ground was dry and did not hold a scent well. A break for the searchers came when heavy thunderstorms covered the area. When the ground is wet and damp, the scent is stronger. After the rain, it took the dogs only three hours to track down James Earl Ray.

Suddenly, Sandy, a fourteen-month-old bloodhound, gently nuzzled the escaped criminal out from under a large pile of leaves where he was hiding. Later, the bloodhounds found all of the other escaped prisoners.

James Earl Ray and the other convicts are just a few of the many people found each year by well-trained bloodhounds. Not all the people found by bloodhounds are criminals. Most are lost children, elderly persons, and hunters.

Bloodhounds were the first dog detectives. Originally, the noble hound was bred for his amazing talent for following a scent trail. No other dog has his keen nose. The bloodhound is one of the oldest dog breeds in the world. The first bloodhound probably lived 2,500 years ago in ancient Rome. Later, the Abbots of St. Hubert's Abbey in western Europe raised the dogs.

The name "bloodhound" came from medieval England. The law said that there could be two kinds of hounds—those owned by the peasants and those owned by the nobility or "blue bloods." Those hounds that belonged to the nobility were called the hounds of the blood or the blooded hounds. Most people agree that this is probably where the name bloodhound originated.

At first, they were used for hunting other animals such as deer. Later, especially in the United States, people began

The bloodhound today is the same noble dog that was cherished by the kings of England and the ancient Romans.

using bloodhounds to track down escaped slaves and criminals.

The instinct to follow a scent shows up in even the youngest puppies. A six-month-old bloodhound can follow a trail for three-quarters of a mile. When a dog handler begins training a bloodhound, he is not training it to follow a scent. He is, however, teaching the dog to pay close attention to the job at hand.

When it is time for a bloodhound to go to work, a heavy leather harness is put on the dog. The harness must be very strong because these dogs are extremely powerful. If the harness were to break, the dog would take off at great speed, nose to the ground, while following his trail. The handler might never catch his dog. A bloodhound off his leash is often a dog gone forever.

Sometimes bloodhounds are trained at night so that they learn to use just their noses, and not their eyes, when following a scent trail.

All people have a scent. As a person walks or runs, the body leaves a trail of invisible scent particles. These particles fall to the ground. This is the scent trail that a bloodhound follows. The bloodhound uses his long, floppy ears to swish up the particles from the ground into his nose chamber. The bloodhound's nose is two million times more sensitive than that of a human.

On a warm, dry day, the scent particles rise six or eight feet into the air. It is very difficult for a bloodhound to follow a trail in weather like this. In cold or damp weather, the particles settle down on the ground, making the dog's

Sergeant Zarifis fastens a heavy leather harness on Quincy.

A powerful bloodhound and his handler work as a team.

job easier. That is why it is difficult for a bloodhound to locate someone in a dry desert and easy to trail a person along the damp forest ground.

Many people think that if a criminal crosses a river, the bloodhound will not be able to track him down. This is not true. Actually, the scent particles will just drip off the criminal when he reaches the other side of the water. It will then be even easier for the bloodhound to find him.

Sergeant James Zarifis of the Malverne, Long Island, New York, police department owns a very famous bloodhound. His name is Patriot John Quincy Adams, but his friends call him Quincy. Sergeant Zarifis will lend Quincy, free of charge, to any police department that needs a bloodhound to find a lost person. Quincy searches mostly for lost children and elderly persons who have wandered away. However, Quincy has also tracked down some dangerous criminals.

In one case, a ski-masked robber had just left the house he had burglarized. The lady who owned the house called the police. Quincy and Sergeant Zarifis arrived at the scene of the crime fifteen hours later. By this time, the trail was not fresh. Quincy went into the house, moving around in circles, looking for a scent.

Suddenly, the bloodhound sniffed excitedly around the windowsill and door. He had found a strong scent.

Quincy pulled Sergeant Zarifis out the door. They went up hills, over fences, and through several backyards. The trail ended on the sidewalk of another street some distance away. Quincy had lost the scent and it seemed like a dead end.

Sergeant Zarifis did not know the importance of Quincy's accomplishment. He later discovered that his bloodhound had stopped across the street from the house of the man whom the police suspected of being the robber.

The bloodhound is so accurate in following a trail that his evidence is accepted in a court of law. Some of the greatest bloodhounds have helped catch more criminals than the best human detectives. One dog actually helped find more than 600 criminals.

Many people are afraid of bloodhounds. In movies, these dogs are often shown howling and snarling as they track down and attack their victims. Nothing could be further from the truth. Bloodhounds are never trained to attack people, only to find them. These sweet, lovable dogs like to give a friendly lick to the criminal when they find him. Bloodhounds also give comfort to the frightened children they find. A pat on the head is the only reward they seek for doing their job.

The bloodhound is an unusual-looking dog. His sad eyes always look as though he is about to cry. His skin is very loose and wrinkled around his head and neck. The smooth coat is usually tan with black or red markings. He can also be a tawny color. He is a very large, powerful animal and can weigh as much as 110 pounds.

Bloodhounds are quiet when trailing. They do not howl or bay while moving through the woods, which is just as well. If the criminal knew the dog was coming, he might try to harm him. A lost child who is already frightened would only be more scared by the sound of a dog coming. The only time a bloodhound barks is when he has found the person he is searching for. He does this to alert the handler to come to help.

A bloodhound and his handler work as a team—one dog and one man. They never work in packs. Some dogs get right on the trail, their noses to the ground. Others will move back and forth across the trail, sometimes jumping into the air to search for scent particles.

Bloodhounds are very stubborn animals. They rarely give up the search unless they lose the scent. One dog followed a scent trail for 138 miles. Another trailed an escaped criminal for more than fifty miles.

One of the most famous bloodhounds of all time was named Nick Carter. He once followed a trail that was 105 hours old. This shows how determined a bloodhound can be.

For a time, people stopped using bloodhounds for tracking because the police were using modern radios and helicopters to do the same job. Yet, in the case of James Earl Ray, the bloodhound proved that he could do what the helicopters could not. Recently, some bloodhound owners have started missing-persons services. They fly around the country, wherever they are needed, to find lost or kidnapped people.

One such group is the Sierra Madre Search and Rescue Team. The team is made up of four dogs and twenty-five men. They travel to many states on rescue missions. Many of the men in the group are doctors, radio operators, and helicopter and airplane pilots. These men are all expert mountain climbers. The dog lives with the man who trains him. He is kept outside most of the time so that he will get accustomed to cold temperatures.

Sergeant Zarifis believes that bloodhounds are not used as much as they should be. In the future, more and more police departments will use the bloodhound's amazing trailing ability as another tool of modern police work.

8

DRUG- AND BOMB-DETECTOR DOGS

It is just another routine workday for Officer Ray O'Leary of the United States Customs Service and his dog Pepper. Officer O'Leary pulls his station wagon onto the New York City docks where endless piles of boxes and bags are stacked high. Large ships from all over the world unload their cargo on these docks.

In the back of the station wagon is a large wire cage. A black-and-tan dog sits patiently in the cage, anxious to begin work. The dog is a female German shepherd with one floppy ear and one straight ear.

Officer O'Leary attaches a sturdy leash to the dog's collar and they go to work. Pepper is led to a high pile of burlap bags. At first, the dog sniffs all around the bags nearest the floor. Then, satisfied that there is nothing there, starts climbing on the large sacks. Higher and higher she climbs, sniffing all the while. Finally, Pepper reaches the very top of the pile. She looks at her handler to make sure he is still there.

Suddenly, the dog stops. She sniffs again at one sack. Pepper becomes very excited. She begins digging with her feet and ripping at the sack with her sharp teeth. Soon, the officer is beside his dog, trying to see what she has found. It is a small, carefully wrapped package of marijuana that a drug smuggler had hidden there.

The Customs Detector Dog Program was started in September 1970. These intelligent and hard-working dogs have become the major tool in fighting the war against narcotics smuggling. In 1979, canine enforcement teams found illegal drugs 7,175 times. If these drugs had been sold, they would have been worth more than 85 million dollars. The smuggled drugs are marijuana, hashish, cocaine, and heroin. They are illegal because they are harmful to the people who take them and can be fatal.

Customs officials are constantly inspecting incoming cargo on docks, in airports, at international mail facilities, and at border-crossing points. These customs detector dogs, working with their handlers, make the overwhelming task of inspection possible. However, these dogs are never used to search people.

The dogs can search packages, cars, and airplanes much faster than people can. For example, 400 to 500 packages would take a customs inspector several days to examine. A detector dog and his handler can do the job in less than thirty minutes. At border crossings, a dog can search a car thoroughly in less than five minutes. A man, working alone, would take at least a half-hour to do the same job.

In the beginning, there were only thirteen dog/man teams. Today, the number has grown to 122. At first, the customs service used dogs trained by the air force. Then, the best air force dog trainers taught the customs officers how to train their own dogs.

Both officers and dogs must be highly qualified to be considered for the Customs Detector Dog Program. The officer must have at least one year of dog-handling experience. The dogs that are selected must be very active and always moving. Actually, the very kind of dog that does not make a good pet often makes the best detector dog.

Many of the dogs chosen are German shepherds and Labrador retrievers. Other breeds, including Brittany spaniels, German short-hair pointers, Irish setters, and Airedales are

Officer F. Urban and his dog Dora search a car for narcotics at a border-crossing point.

also used. Sometimes, mutts or mixed breeds are picked for the job.

The dogs selected are usually two to three years old. Most come from animal shelters and would have been destroyed if they had not qualified for customs work. Also, many people give their dogs to the Customs Service because they want to help fight the growing drug-smuggling problem. Even so, only one out of every 130 dogs is lucky enough to be selected. Only the most energetic dogs, with a good sense of smell, can be used.

A specially selected dog and a handler are paired at the Detector Dog Training Center in Fort Royal, Virginia. Here, the dog and handler are taught to work as a team.

The training lasts for twenty weeks. The dog is taught to use his keen sense of smell to sniff out hidden narcotics. The handler is taught to understand the dog. First, the dog learns basic obedience so that the handler can manage him. Next, the dog learns to retrieve objects that smell like the narcotic.

The dog is trained to use his teeth or feet to show that he has found the drug. To do this, the drug is hidden in a "training aid." This is usually a rolled-up towel tied with tape. Each time the dog retrieves the training aid, the handler plays a game with him called "roughhouse." It is like playing tug-of-war with the rolled-up towel. The game gets rougher and rougher until the dog gets very angry with the towel and the drug hidden inside it.

Soon, the dog learns to search entire buildings. He is taught to search boxes, cars, and airplanes. By the time this part of the training is completed, the detector dog can easily locate marijuana and hashish. The second part of the training teaches him to find cocaine and heroin.

Before the handler and his dog can graduate, they must pass very difficult tests that last for several days. During these tests, the dog must find all types of drugs hidden in many strange places. In one test, the dog checks both the insides and outsides of cars and trucks. The dog must be able to find the drugs and show his handler exactly where they are hidden. The team must achieve a perfect score. If they do not do everything correctly, they will fail.

After the dog and his handler graduate, training continues. Each day, the handler and dog practice the lessons they have learned so that they will never forget how to do their job well. The teams are sent to different places to practice. They practice searching for drugs in warehouses, mailrooms, airports, airplanes, and ships. When the dogs search

During a training session, Nat locates six pounds of cocaine hidden in the rim of a tire.

in mailrooms and airports, they must jump up on a moving conveyor belt. This way, they can examine more boxes and pieces of baggage in a shorter period of time.

The handler and his dog become very close friends. Actually, they are partners that work together until one or the other retires. These hard-working, talented dogs stay on the job until they are about nine years old. They all retire with honors. Most move in with their handler and his family, others may go to new households.

One special dog named Chopper worked until he was twelve years old. This canine drug-sniffer found more than 80 million dollars worth of smuggled narcotics during his ten-year career with the Customs Service. Chopper now lives with his handler.

One of the most famous customs dogs was a German shepherd named Bob. When he had finished training, he was sent to work at a border-crossing point between Texas and Mexico. During Bob's career, he located drugs 970 times. His largest find was 580 pounds of marijuana that had been cleverly concealed in a car.

Another talented customs dog named Duke discovered 225 pounds of hashish in a camper that had been sent to Boston, Massachusetts. The value of the drug would have been $300,000 by the time it was sold illegally on the streets.

One of the biggest finds was by Officer Mike Burns and his dog Scorpio. While checking luggage at Miami International Airport, they discovered a suitcase containing seventy-five pounds of cocaine. The cocaine was worth 16 million dollars.

Since the Customs Service first started using these special dogs, the smugglers have become worried. Some have tried almost every imaginable way to keep the dogs from finding the drugs. They have covered the drugs with perfume and ammonia, hidden them in rolled-up carpets, and wrapped them in plastic bags, to name a few schemes. The dogs seem to be winning, as there is no way to really hide the smell of narcotics from a good detector dog.

In April of 1980, the United States Customs Service celebrated the tenth anniversary of the Drug Detector Dog Program. The wonderful, drug-sniffing dogs have made a major contribution in the war against drug smuggling.

Bomb-sniffing dogs have also worked hard to serve mankind. Although very advanced, scientific bomb-sniffing instruments have been invented, they are not the whole answer to the problem. These machines are expensive to make, very delicate, and cannot be easily moved from place to place. The very best bomb-finder today is man's best and oldest friend—the dog. These talented canines are now being used all over the country by police departments, airport police, and the military.

On May 1, 1971, the New York City Police Department Bomb Squad got their first two bomb-detector dogs. Brandy, a German shepherd, and Sally, a Labrador retriever, were to be part of an experimental program.

Brandy and Sally were trained to detect explosives by the psychology department of the University of Mississippi under a federal grant. Both dogs had received basic obedience training. They were used to working both on and off a leash and with more than one handler.

All bomb-detector dogs must first learn to recognize the odor of explosives such as dynamite, smokeless and black powders, C-4 (a plastic explosive), and others. This is the most important lesson for the dog to learn. Each time the dog does his job, he is rewarded with food and praise.

Next, the bomb dogs learn how to search a room on command. When a handler says "Search," the dog sniffs curiously around the room. He is eager to find an explosive, for he knows it means a reward of food. These dogs are successful 95 percent of the time.

Bomb-detector dogs must be very calm. Unlike drug detector dogs, they sit quietly when they find what they are looking for and never bark or jump around. If they did that, they might set off a bomb.

These dogs are also a timesaving tool. This is especially true when a cluttered area, such as an office or airport terminal, is to be searched for explosives. The dog's smelling ability helps him to find a bomb when a man might easily overlook it if it is cleverly hidden. When a dog finds a bomb, he is taught to sit, facing away from the bomb. In this way, the handler knows his dog has found something with an explosive odor.

In March of 1972, Brandy proved that the experiment had succeeded. An airborne 707 jetliner was called back to John F. Kennedy International Airport in New York when a man telephoned to say that there was a bomb on board. An airplane has many small places where a bomb could be easily concealed. Brandy was brought into the plane to search. In less than a minute, Brandy sat down and turned to her handler as if to say, "I've done my job." The bomb was concealed in a briefcase in the cockpit of the plane. Brandy saved many lives that day.

The New York City Police Department now has seven bomb dogs. They have been used in subways and on ships, in vehicles and in hotels. They have also been used at both the Democratic and Republican National Conventions to make sure that there were no hidden bombs.

Bomb-detector dogs have also been used by the Secret Service to search the White House. Through it all, the bomb dogs have done everything that their human masters have asked of them, and more.

9

FRIEND AND COMPANION

It is a quiet, still night in the children's ward of the hospital. The room where several children sleep is dark. All of the children are asleep, except one. The seven-year-old girl had just arrived that day. She is huddled in a round ball under the bedcovers. She cries and cries because she is lonely. Her mother and father are not allowed to stay in the hospital with her. This girl is emotionally disturbed. She will have to stay in the hospital for a while, until the doctors can help her.

Suddenly, a cold, wet nose nuzzles under the blanket, searching for the girl's hand. The child is frightened at first and jumps. Then, she realizes that the nose belongs to a big dog. She is surprised to find a real dog in a hospital. The dog's name is Skeezer, and she is the hospital's dog.

Slowly, Skeezer crawls up onto the bed with the sad, little girl. She cuddles close against the child's shaking body. The friendly warmth of the big, black dog feels good. Soon, the girl stops crying. She hugs Skeezer close and sighs. Together, they both fall asleep.

Skeezer is a real dog who lives at the Children's Psychiatric Hospital in Ann Arbor, Michigan. The doctors and nurses who work there call her a "canine therapist." Skeezer's special task is to help emotionally disturbed children. She is very good at her job.

Even when the doctors can't comfort the lonely, frightened children, Skeezer can. A wet, doggy kiss and a big, black paw reach some children in ways that no human could. Skeezer only asks to be loved in return. She is able to tell when a child needs someone to love, hug, and talk to. Skeezer always has time to listen when the children speak to her. She turns her furry head this way and that, as if she understands exactly what they are saying. Perhaps she does.

Skeezer may be the first dog in the country to be used for this purpose. Man has come to realize that dogs of all sizes and breeds can help people, both children and adults, with their problems.

In the children's ward of another hospital in California, a shaggy English sheep dog roams the halls. He looks for sick children who are frightened at being away from home, family, and friends. This dog also gives them love and extra attention. He makes their hospital stay a little less frightening.

Recently, it was discovered that dogs are also able to aid recovering heart-attack patients. It is important to have a loving dog waiting for these people when they come home from the hospital. They know that their dog depends upon them for everything—food, shelter, and most of all, love. The dogs seem to give the people something to live for. Although science cannot explain why, those patients who have dogs live longer than those who do not. The use of dogs in this way is called "pet-facilitated therapy."

Dogs can be a great help to elderly people who live alone and do not get out much. When a senior citizen is given a dog, the change in his or her way of life is remarkable. Suddenly, the person will be out walking to the supermarket to buy pet food. Along the way, he or she will begin meeting and speaking with people again.

In Los Angeles, California, dogs are used to make delinquent teenagers feel better about themselves. The teenagers are taught to train their pets to heel, sit, and stay. When the training is done, two things have happened. Firstly, the dogs are very well-behaved. Secondly, the teenagers are proud that they have accomplished something.

During the training, the teenagers also learn to understand and love their pets. Often, this helps them to get along better with people as well. It is clear that the strong bond of friendship between a person and a dog can help one to become more loving and kind to all people.

Jay Meranchik, Director of the Feeling Heart Foundation, also believes that dogs can help people. He taught his German shepherd, Natasha, and Doberman pinscher, Cho, some simple tricks. Then, he took the dogs to visit people in hospitals, nursing homes, and special schools. At first, many hospital employees didn't let the dogs inside because they thought that they carry germs. However, when they saw how much the patients enjoyed the dogs, they changed their minds.

Natasha and Cho are taken wherever they are needed. In classrooms, the two large dogs perform their tricks at the children's commands. The children are so pleased that they can control the dogs, they begin to learn to better control themselves.

Natasha's greatest success came when she was playing with a little girl who had a speech problem. Natasha refused to bark until the child could clearly say "Speak." For fifteen minutes she tried to say the word. She just couldn't. Natasha waited patiently, watching the child. Finally, after much struggling, the girl said "Speak." When Natasha barked loudly, the girl was thrilled. In her own way, Natasha taught her to do something that even the teachers had been unable to teach her.

Today, we discover more ways in which faithful dogs help mankind. They are truly our best friend. A man named George Graham Vest put into words his appreciation of the dog's contribution. He said:

> The one absolutely unselfish friend that man can have in this selfish world, the one that never deserts him, the one that never proves ungrateful or treacherous, is his dog. A man's dog stands by him in prosperity and in poverty, in health and in sickness. He will sleep on the cold ground, when the wintry winds blow and the snow drives fiercely, if only he may be

near his master's side. He will kiss the hand that has no food to offer; he will lick the wounds and sores that come in encounters with the roughness of the world. He guards the sleep of his pauper master, as if he were a prince. When all other friends desert, he remains . . . and when the last scene of all comes and death takes the master in its embrace and the body is laid away in the cold ground, no matter if all other friends pursue their way, there by the graveside will the noble dog be found, his head between his paws, his eyes sad, but open in watchfulness, faithful and true even in death.

One of the most famous and touching examples of man's special relationship with dogs occurred in Edinburgh, Scotland. In 1858, a man named John Gray died. As the funeral procession moved from the church to Greyfriars' Cemetery, the man's little dog followed. The dog was a shaggy, little Skye terrier named Bobby.

The next morning, people were surprised to see the little dog lying beside his master's grave. Since dogs were not allowed there, he was thrown out. The next morning, Bobby was back again. Once more, he was made to leave. On the third morning, Bobby returned. This time, the people felt sorry for him and let the little dog stay.

From that day on, Bobby rarely left his master's grave. He went only to a restaurant where he and his master used to go for their afternoon meal. The proprietor always gave the little dog some scraps. As soon as Bobby finished eating, he

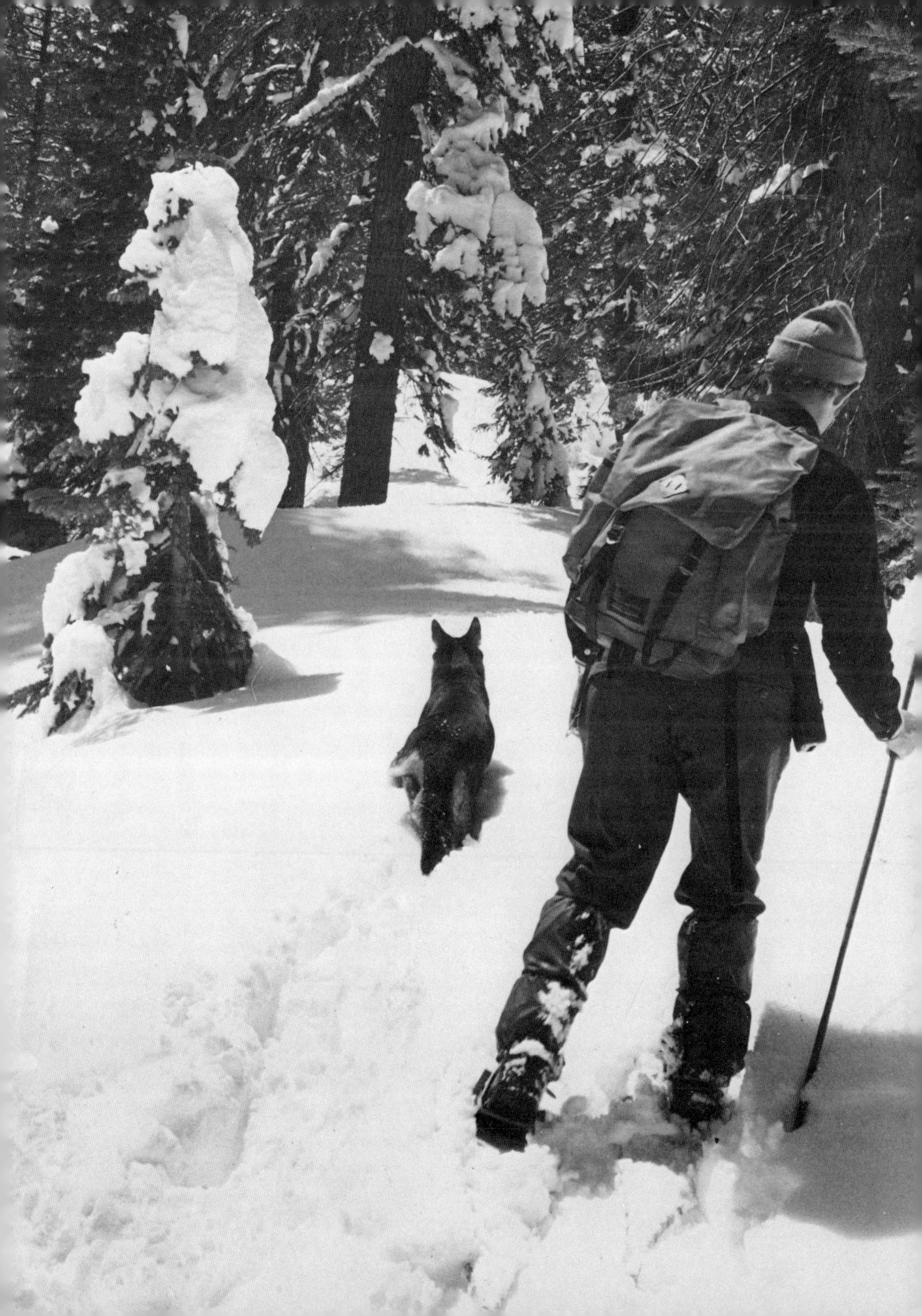

would return to the cemetery, carrying a scrap of food with him.

For fourteen years, Bobby's routine never changed, and he became known as Greyfriars' Bobby. His loyalty to his master, John Gray, continued until the little dog became old and sick.

Bobby has become part of the history of Edinburgh. The townspeople were so impressed with his show of love that they erected a monument to the little Skye terrier. It stands there to this day. It is a constant reminder that dogs love and need man as much as he loves and needs them.

INDEX

Afgan, 25
Airedale, 79
Alaska, 27-28, 29, 30, 32
Alaskan Malamute, 29, 30-32
All Alaska Sweepstakes, 29
American Humane
 Association, 42
American Rescue Dog
 Association, 51, 55
Ann Arbor (Michigan), 87
Australia, 64

Bloodhound, 68-76
 history of, 69
 Nick Carter, 75
 Patriot John Quincy
  Adams, 73-74
Bomb-Detector Dogs, 77-85
 training of, 83-84
Boxer, 37
Brittany Spaniel, 79
Brushy Mountain State
 Prison (Tennessee), 68
Burns, Mike, 82
Byrd, Admiral Richard, 32

Canada, 24, 32, 33, 62, 63
Central Park (New York
 City), 28
Chesapeake Bay Retriever, 64
Children's Psychiatric
 Hospital (Ann Arbor,
 Michigan), 87
Collie, 37
Companion Dogs, 86-92
 Skeezer, 86-87
Coonhound, 25
Customs Detector Dog
 Program, 78, 79, 83

Dachshund, 18-19
Detective Dogs, 17, 68-76
Detector Dog Training
 Center, 80
Doberman Pinschers, 88
 Cho, 88-89

Dogs
 as guards, 15-17
 in ancient Egypt, 15
 in ancient Rome, 63-64, 69
 on the Mayflower, 21

93

Drug-Detector Dogs, 77-85
   Chopper, 82
   Duke, 82
   Scorpio, 82
   training of, 80-81

Edinburgh (Scotland), 90, 92
England, 21, 62, 64, 69
English Setter, 24
English Sheep Dog, 87
Epilepsy (dogs aid victims of), 43-44
Eustis, Mrs. Dorothy H., 36

Farm Dogs, 15-17
   Herding Dogs, 17
Feeling Heart Foundation, 88
Foxhound, 25
France, 47, 62, 64
Frank, Morris S., 36
Franklin, Benjamin, 21

German Shepherd, 36, 37, 51, 56, 77, 79, 82, 83, 88
   Bob, 82
   Brandy, 83, 84-85
   Natasha, 88-89
   Pepper, 77-78
German Short-Haired Pointer, 24, 79
Germany, 35

Golden Lab, 38
Golden Retriever, 37, 38
Gordon Setter, 24
Gray, John, 90-92
Greenland, 33
Greyhound, 21, 25
Guide Dog Foundation for the Blind, 38, 40

Hearing-Ear Dogs, 35-44
   best types of dogs for, 42
   training for, 42
Holland, 63
Hounds, 21, 24-26
Hunting Dogs, 14-15, 18-26
   Clary, 18-19

Irish Setter, 24, 79
Italy, 47

Klondike Gold Rush, 32

Labrador, 33
Labrador Retriever, 24, 35, 38, 40, 62, 79, 83
   Sally, 83
Landseer, Sir Edwin, 63
Lifesaving Dogs, 61-67
Los Angeles (California), 88

Mastiff, 21
Meranchik, Jay, 88
Mount St. Helens, 56

Napoleon, 64
New York City, 77, 84
New York City Police Department, 83, 85
New York State, 18, 43
Newfoundland (Canada), 24, 63
Newfoundland Dogs (Newfs), 62-67
  in ancient Rome, 63-64
  Landseer, 63
  water training for, 64-67
Newfoundland Club of America, 64
North Pole, 32

O'Leary, Ray, 77

Peary, Robert, 32
Pointers, 21, 23, 79

Ray, James Earl, 68-69, 75
Retrievers, 21, 23-24. *Also see* Labrador Retrievers, Chesapeake Bay Retrievers.

Russian Samoyed, 29, 30

St. Bernard, 47-48
  Barry, 48
Search and Rescue Dogs, 45-60
  training for, 51-55, 56
Seeing-Eye Dogs, 17, 35-44
  best breeds for, 37
  history of, 35-36
  Ingrid, 35
  organizations for training, 36
  training of, 38-40
Setters, 21, 23, 24, 79
Siberia, 29, 30
Siberian Husky, 27, 29, 32
Sierra Madre Search and Rescue Team, 75-76
Skye Terrier, 90-92
Sled Dogs, 27-34
  Balto, 27-28
South Pole, 32
Spain, 62
Spaniels, 21, 23, 79
Springer Spaniel, 21
Swanton, Ernest, 40
Swiss Alps, 45, 48
Switzerland, 36, 45, 51

Terriers, 19-20, 90-92
  Bobby, 90-92
Therapy Dogs, 86-88

95

United States Custom Service, 77, 80, 82, 83

Vest, George Graham, 89

Whippets, 25-26
White House, 85
Windsor Castle, 64

Zarifis, Sergeant James, 73-74, 76